THE

FACTOR

AMY G. PHILIPP

WESTBOW
PRESS®
A DIVISION OF THOMAS NELSON
& ZONDERVAN

WestBow Press books may be ordered through booksellers or by contacting:

WestBow Press
A Division of Thomas Nelson & Zondervan
1663 Liberty Drive
Bloomington, IN 47403
www.westbowpress.com
844-714-3454

ISBN: 978-1-6642-5058-1 (sc)
ISBN: 978-1-6642-5059-8 (e)

Library of Congress Control Number: 2021923749

Print information available on the last page.

WestBow Press rev. date: 12/09/2021

Foreword

I keep asking that the God of our Lord Jesus Christ, the glorious Father, may give you the Spirit of wisdom and revelation, so that you may know him better. (Ephesians 1:17 NIV)

Dedication

This book was written with the hope that all who read it will discover the abundant benefits extended to those who place and embrace their identities in Jesus Christ.

Acknowledgements

First and foremost, I am thankful to God for His holy Word, my access to it, and the grace by which I have been saved. I'm extremely grateful to Kenisha Bethea for her keen eye and editing expertise, and I'm eternally thankful for all the Bible study leaders and pastors whom God equipped to teach and share His Word with me and others over the years. I also sincerely appreciate God's provision in myriad ways and the love and support of my husband, all of which enabled me to take a professional hiatus and write. Additionally, I extend special thanks and recognition to my daughter, A.B. Moore, who created the cover design.

Identity—A Timeless Topic

As a pre-teen, I had a strong desire to possess a trendy item—a Speidel identity bracelet. Ads on tv at the time marketed them as Speidel "Idents," and I was thrilled to receive one for my birthday. My signature bracelet was gold, and my initials were engraved on a thin bar that crested the top of my wrist. It was my first "real" piece of jewelry, and I wore it every day.

As I recall my desire to have my identity labeled in wearable form, I've come to realize that keen interest in the concept of personal identity and its exploration never seem to go out of style. Think of all the personality surveys and assessments that abound. I've enjoyed taking many of them over the years and discovering my innate traits as well as what naturally motivates me.

But it's not just me. In the last few years, articles and posts about identity have appeared on my news and social media feeds more and more frequently. Could it be because the topic of *self* resonates with most human beings? I think so. Many people are actively seeking to understand, label and share their personal identities based on myriad traits, feelings and factors.

As I contemplated this topic, it occurred to me how foundational and transformational it is to understand one's identity in Jesus Christ, and how this one particular type of identity transcends all others. So, as a sequel to *The SQ Factor*, which explored the importance of spiritual intelligence as opposed to IQ and EQ (cognitive intelligence and emotional intelligence), *The ID Factor* will explore God's Word and provide opportunities to personally process and understand what identity in Jesus Christ is as well as discover its infinite benefits.

What is Identity in Christ - A Personal Discovery

When I was in high school, my mother started attending what many may call a *Bible-preaching* church. It was very different from the formal, liturgical church I grew up attending, and it was quite interesting to hear how much my mother enjoyed going and sharing about it—especially when my church experiences up to that point had been much the opposite.

Although there were aspects of my childhood church that I liked, such as my fourth-grade Sunday school teacher—an older gentleman who enjoyed teaching and being around kids—and the after-service lollipops provided by another older congregant, I honestly can't say that I loved going to church.

For one, I was a tomboy, and I hated wearing a dress, stockings, and patent leather shoes—all somewhat of an unspoken dress code for women and girls at my childhood church. I made it through the formal services by doodling on the scribble pad provided in the pews for children. In addition to the fashion expectations, my middle school confirmation experience also served to reinforce my less than positive attitude about church.

During that time, I was *graded* on my morning Sunday school attendance. (I got a C!) We also had to take tests that assessed what we learned in additional Sunday afternoon classes. I distinctly remember having to define words like *propitiation* and *atonement*. The point is, none of the required confirmation work helped me to understand God or actively grow in my faith. Through the confirmation process requirements, I gathered lots of doctrinal and denominational "head" knowledge, but I didn't develop any "heart" knowledge of God.

As I processed these memories over the years, I realized that the fond childhood recollections I had of church were the relational memories of special people who had a heart for teaching, reaching, and interacting with others. They did what they did voluntarily. They weren't told that they had to do it, and their service wasn't *required*. I also came to understand that the unspoken cultural, denominational "rules" of my particular childhood church just weren't a match for my personality or learning style. They affected my perception and understanding of the institution of church and why one would want to go.

Things changed one afternoon in high school when I was chatting with my mother. She took the opportunity to talk about her growing faith, not church, and she shared the gospel—the basic, universal, and relational message of the Christian faith. In a nutshell, she helped me to understand that none of us is perfect. Whether large or small in scope, we all do or say things that we shouldn't do, and/or we fail to do things that we should do. Simply put, we all fail to display consistent, exemplary behavior in myriad ways, and none of us can earn forgiveness or a "pass" from our inherent sin nature in and of ourselves. It can only be achieved through the conscious acknowledgment and acceptance of God's free, sacrificial gift of His Son, Jesus Christ, and His grace-based plan for forgiving our shortcomings.

Exploring God's Word about the Gospel

(Author's note: *The ID Factor* was designed to be interactive and participatory. Many of the sections below are written in a format that allows for you to read specific, written verses from the Bible and personally process how they resonate with you. Questions are posed and commentary is provided after you consider what your own takeaways may be.)

Logos
(What God's Word, as Written in the Bible, Shares)

for all have sinned and fall short of the glory of God, and all are justified freely by his grace through the redemption that came by Christ Jesus. (Romans 3:23–24 NIV)

If you declare with your mouth, "Jesus is Lord," and believe in your heart that God raised him from the dead, you will be saved. For it is with your heart that you believe and are justified, and it is with your mouth that you profess your faith and are saved. (Romans 10:9–10 NIV)

for, "Everyone who calls on the name of the Lord will be saved." (Romans 10:13 NIV)

What Are Your Rhema Takeaways? (How Do These Verses Resonate with You?)

Dig Deeper

Logos

For what the *law* was powerless to do because it was weakened by the flesh, God did by sending his own Son in the likeness of sinful flesh to be a sin offering. And so he condemned sin in the flesh. (Romans 8:3 NIV; emphasis mine)

Research Mosaic law. Among its components are the Ten Commandments. Identify the Ten Commandments. (You can Google them or open a Bible to find them in Exodus 20.)

Have you been able to keep all of them?

What do you think the purposes of the various Old Testament laws and commandments were?

What did people do in the Old Testament to atone for various sins?

Logos

> For no one can ever be made right with God by doing what the law commands. The law simply shows us how sinful we are. (Romans 3:20 NLT)

> What then shall we say? That the law is sin? By no means! Yet if it had not been for the law, I would not have known sin. For I would not have known what it is to covet if the law had not said, "You shall not covet." (Romans 7:7 ESV)

What Are Your Rhema Takeaways?

How does the law reveal a knowledge of sin? (You may wish to Google other translations of the verses above. Different translations or versions of the Bible can often provide a better understanding of Scripture.)

Logos

> Do not think that I have come to abolish the *Law of the Prophets*; I have come not to abolish them but to **fulfill** them. (Matthew 5:17 ESV; emphasis mine)

> Behold, the days are coming, declares the LORD, when I will make a **new covenant** with the house of Israel and the house of Judah, (Jeremiah 31:31 ESV; emphasis mine)

> for this is my blood, which confirms the **covenant** between God and his people. It is poured out for many as a sacrifice to forgive the sins of many." (Matthew 26:28 NLT; emphasis mine)

Which verse above is from the Old Testament?

Which ones are from the New Testament?

What is the new covenant?

How is the new covenant different from the law presented in the Old Testament?

Who represents the new covenant?

Embracing the Gospel-The Starting Point for Identifying with Christ

Once I grasped the simple message of the gospel, I realized that going to church, rotely participating in the service, and memorizing terms did not *relationally* connect me to God or make me a Christian. Such actions may have identified me *culturally* as a Christian in regard to faith traditions, but they didn't connect my heart to God.

Understanding and embracing God's plan for redemption through Jesus Christ helped me recognize that there was nothing that I could do or had to do to earn God's forgiveness or favor. There was nothing I could or had to accomplish on my own. Salvation and redemption were all *God's* doing, not *my* doing, as I could never perfectly please God. As the following verse shares, "For it is by grace you have been saved, through faith—and this is not from yourselves, it is the gift of God—not by works, so that no one can boast" (Ephesians 2:8–9 NIV).

This heightened awareness of my spiritual disconnectedness helped me realize that the Christian faith is about a *personal relationship* with God rather than a *religion*, or what Merriam-Webster defines as an "institutionalized system of religious attitudes, beliefs, and practices." I now understood my **identity in Christ**. I am a sinner saved and forgiven. This unique recognition could be described as a *born-again* experience.

The born-again phrase is misunderstood and often maligned by many in our current culture, but it simply means that I grasped things in a new way that penetrated my heart, mind, and soul. By verbally accepting God's grace-based plan for forgiveness, I now had a relational connection to God that transcended jumping through different kinds of man-made, denominational hoops. My faith was no longer a familial, cultural tradition. My relationship with God was personal and elective, and little did I know at the time that my new identity in Christ would include unexpected benefits that were immediate, transformational, and enduring.

Exploring God's Word about Spiritual Rebirth

Logos

for you have been born again [that is, reborn from above—*spiritually transformed, renewed,* and set apart for His purpose] not of seed which is perishable but [from that which is] imperishable and immortal, that is, through the living and everlasting word of God. (1 Peter 1:23 AMP; emphasis mine)

But to all who believed him and accepted him, he gave the right to become children of God. They are *reborn*—not with a physical birth resulting from human passion or plan, but a birth that comes from God. (John 1:12–13 NLT; emphasis mine)

That which is born of the flesh is flesh; and that which is born of the Spirit is spirit. (John 3:6 KJV)

What Are Your Rhema Takeaways?

Do you have a new understanding of the term *born again*? If so, how would you describe it?

Exploring the MANY Benefits of Identity in Christ

As I began exploring the benefits of embracing one's identity in Jesus Christ, I realized that the well is deep! It's exciting to share all the promises and blessings extended to *believers*. For organizational and processing purposes, we'll divide them into three categories: **Immediate Benefits**, **Transformational Benefits**, and **Enduring Benefits**.

IMMEDIATE BENEFITS

1. Inclusion and Security

Logos

> And you also were **included** in Christ when you heard the message of truth, the gospel of your salvation. When you believed, you were **marked in him with**

a seal, the promised Holy Spirit, who is a **deposit guaranteeing our inheritance** until the redemption of those who are God's possession—to the praise of his glory. (Ephesians 1:13–14 NIV; emphasis mine)

What Are Your Rhema Takeaways?

These verses are rich with assurances. First, we are *allies* with Christ! Second, He has given us a seal. Seals were used historically to ensure the safety or validity of the contents of a letter, and often they had specific lettering, perhaps an identifying monogram. Third, when believers accept Jesus Christ as Savior, they immediately receive a deposit or down payment, the Holy Spirit, who guarantees the security of their future.

2. Non-discriminatory Unity

Logos

So in Christ Jesus, *you are all children of God through faith*, for all of you who were baptized into Christ have clothed yourselves with Christ. There is neither Jew nor Greek, there is neither male nor female;

for you are all one in Christ Jesus. (Galatians 3:26-28 NIV; emphasis mine)

Now you are the **body of Christ and individually members** of it. (1 Corinthians 12:27, ESV; emphasis mine)

But we are **citizens of heaven**, where the Lord Jesus Christ lives. And we are eagerly waiting for him to return as our Savior. (Philippians 3:20 NLT; emphasis mine)

But he who is joined to the Lord becomes **one spirit** with him. (1 Corinthians 6:17 ESV; emphasis mine)

What Are Your Rhema Takeaways?

A believer's identity in Christ is not based upon race, gender or nationality. We are part of a family, but our individuality is recognized. We are united with Christ, and we have citizenship in heaven. In light of the many, current sociological issues and the divisiveness that abounds in the world, these verses are especially enlightening and encouraging to me.

3. Personal Help and Instruction

Logos

> But the **Helper**, the **Holy Spirit,** whom
> the Father will send in My name, He will
> **teach you** all things and remind you of
> all that I said to you. (John 14:26 NASB;
> emphasis mine)

> And I will ask the Father, and he will
> **give** you another Helper, that **He may
> be with you forever**, even **the Spirit of
> truth**. **whom the world cannot receive**,
> because it neither sees him nor knows him.
> You know him, for he dwells with you
> and will be in you. (John 14:16-17 ESV;
> emphasis mine)

What Are Your Rhema Takeaways?

God will assist us in getting to know Him, and He will help
us understand His will and His ways as well as what is right
and wrong. Believers will not be abandoned. The gift of the
Holy Spirit is exclusive to believers.

Dig Deeper

Who comprises the Holy Trinity? You may wish to look-up Matthew 28:19 or Luke 3:22, two verses that provide helpful insight and clarity.

4. Life Redefined

Logos

> But these are written that you may believe that Jesus is the Messiah, the Son of God, and that by believing **you may have life in his name**. (John 20:31 NIV; emphasis mine)

> For those who find me find life and receive **favor** from the LORD. (Proverbs 8:35 NIV)

What Are Your Rhema Takeaways?

The life that believers have in Christ is spiritual. It involves our hearts and our souls. How is our physical life different? How does the promise of favor make you feel?

Logos

> For God so loved the world that he gave his one and only Son, that whoever believes in him shall not perish but have *eternal life*. For God did not send his Son into the world to condemn the world, but to save the world through him. (John 3:16–17 NIV; emphasis mine)

> For the wages of sin is death, but the gift of God is eternal life through Jesus Christ our Lord. (Romans 6:23 KJV)

What Are Your Rhema Takeaways?

5. Access, Care and Provision

Logos

> This is the **confidence** we have in approaching God: that if we ask anything **according to his will**, **he hears us**. (1 John 5:14 NIV; emphasis mine)

> **Ask** and it will be **given** to you; **seek** and you will **find**; **knock** and the **door** will

be **opened** to you. For everyone who asks **receives**; the one who seeks **finds**; and to the one who knocks, the **door will be opened**. (Matthew 7:7–8 NIV)

If you remain in me and my words remain in you, ask whatever you wish, and it will be done for you. (John 15:7 NIV; emphasis mine)

What are your Rhema Takeaways?

God wants to reveal things to us! He's given us an invitation to ask and look. God is welcoming and responsive to our questions. Embracing God's Word and actively applying it in our daily lives leads to the blessing of God's care and provision.

6. Exclusive, Personal Gifts

Logos

There are different kinds of **spiritual gifts**, but the same Spirit is the source of them all. (1 Corinthians 12:4 NLT; emphasis mine)

A spiritual gift is given to each of us so we can help each other. To one person the Spirit gives the ability to give **wise advice**; to another the same Spirit gives a message of **special knowledge**. The same Spirit gives **great faith** to another, and to someone else the one Spirit gives the **gift of healing**. He gives one person the **power to perform miracles**, and another the **ability to prophesy**. He gives someone else the **ability to discern** whether a message is from the Spirit of God or from another spirit. Still another person is given the ability to **speak in unknown languages**, while another is given the **ability to interpret** what is being said. (1 Corinthians 12:7–10 NLT)

What are your Rhema Takeaways?

As believers, we are blessed with various forms of unique gifts from the Holy Spirit. The purpose of those gifts is to help others. Spiritual gifts develop and mature as believers draw closer to The Lord and learn His Word and internalize His will and ways.

Dig Deeper

Do you know what your spiritual gift(s) may be? There are different inventories and assessments that you can take for free online. What immediate benefits come to mind about knowing your spiritual gifts?

Spiritual Transformation

While it is encouraging to know that believers receive immediate benefits upon embracing Jesus Christ as Savior, there are other benefits that one could say accumulate interest and are honed and refined over time. This is because learning to internalize God's Word and will and ways is a developmental process. The benefits of such growth occur through practical application, experiential learning and putting faith into action. The following Scripture sheds light on this: "Brothers and sisters, I could not address you as people who live by the Spirit but as people who are still worldly—mere infants in Christ. I gave you milk, not solid food, for you were not yet ready for it. Indeed, you are still not ready." (I Corinthians 3:1-2 NIV)

My faith journey could be described as taking one step forward and two steps backwards. As a young, new Christian, I lacked perspective, discipline and maturity (and a whole lot of other things), which affected my ability to fully trust God and devote time to prayer and Bible study. My spiritual growth was hindered because it took me a while to develop a desire and a taste for deeper Christian community and involvement. Fortunately, God is omniscient and His Word shares that He is cognizant of the spiritual growth process.

Logos

> For by a single offering He has perfected for all time those who are *being sanctified*. (Hebrews 10:14 ESV; emphasis mine)

> God's law was given so that all people could see how sinful they were. But as people sinned more and more, God's wonderful grace became more abundant. (Romans 5:20 NLT)

> But he gives us more grace. That is why Scripture says: "God opposes the proud but shows favor to the humble." (James 4:6 NIV)

> Because of the LORD's great love we are not consumed, for his *compassions never fail*. They are *new every morning*; *great is your faithfulness*. (Lamentations 3:22–23 NIV; emphasis mine)

> If we are unfaithful, he remains **faithful**, for he cannot deny who he is. (2 Timothy 2:13 NLT; emphasis mine)

What Are Your Rhema Takeaways?

Words simply cannot express how grateful I am for God's patience, faithfulness, mercy and grace over the years when I owned my myriad shortcomings and asked for forgiveness. I truly regret that I didn't understand that obedience to Christ was not a burden, but instead, it came with peace, protection, wisdom, provision and blessings. The following is an exploration of some of the transformational blessings, or benefits, of choosing to place your identity in Christ first and foremost.

TRANSFORMATIONAL BENEFITS OF IDENTITY IN CHRIST

1. A New Heart and Spirit

Logos

> This means that anyone who belongs to Christ has become a **new person**. The old life is gone; a new life has begun! (2 Corinthians 5:17 NLT; emphasis mine)

> I will give you a **new heart and put a new spirit** in you; I will remove from you your heart of stone and give you a heart

of flesh. And I will put my Spirit in you and move you to follow my decrees and be careful to keep my laws. (Ezekiel 36:26–27 NIV; emphasis mine)

And do not grieve the Holy Spirit of God, by whom you were sealed for the day of redemption. (Ephesians 4:30 NIV)

What Are Your Rhema Takeaways?

Some of the choices that I made over the years that weren't aligned with God's precepts adversely affected my holistic well-being. Because I had the conviction of the Holy Spirit within me, I understood and tangibly felt the palpable impact of making choices and decisions that were self-serving or that were just blatantly disobedient to what I knew was right. Over time, I learned that my inner peace was directly related to staying connected to God and letting Him lead. Let's just say it got old having to confess, or own up, to things that I thought, said or did that were offensive or disrespectful to God.

Logos

But thanks be to God that, though you used to be slaves to sin, you have come to *obey from your heart* the pattern of teaching that has now claimed your allegiance. (Romans 6:17 NIV; emphasis mine)

What Is Your Rhema Takeaway?

2. Improved Character

Logos

I am the true vine, and my Father is the gardener. He cuts off every branch in me that bears no fruit, while every branch that does bear fruit he prunes so that it will be even more fruitful. You are already clean because of the word I have spoken to you. Remain in me, as I also remain in you. No branch can bear fruit by itself; it must remain in the vine. Neither can you bear fruit unless you remain in me. (John 15:1–4 NIV)

But the Holy Spirit produces this kind of fruit in our lives: love, joy, peace, patience, kindness, goodness, faithfulness, (Galatians 5:22 NLT)

What Are Your Rhema Takeaways?

Staying connected to the vine, Jesus, requires seeking, learning, knowing and applying God's Word as well as connecting with God through prayer on a consistent basis. Such pursuits are the fertilizers of faith. When believers properly care for their spiritual lives, very specific, healthy qualities will emerge and become evident to others.

3. Humility

Logos

> This is what the LORD says: "Let not the wise boast of their wisdom or the strong boast of their strength, or the rich boast of their riches, **but let the one who boasts boast about this: that they have the understanding to know me, that I am the LORD**, who exercises kindness, justice and righteousness on earth, for in these I delight," declares the LORD.(Jeremiah 9:23–24 NIV; emphasis mine)

> Humble yourselves before the Lord, and he will lift you up. (James 4:10 NIV)

He guides the humble in what is right and teaches them his way. (Psalm 25:9 NIV)

What Are Your Rhema Takeaways?

The Lord is able to instruct those with a teachable spirit, and respectability is a by-product of humility. Having a spirit of humility is not something that comes naturally to most human beings. Many of the messages of our culture promote individual, group or corporate pride, which is the antithesis of humility. As I considered what Scripture shares about pride and humility, it occurred to me how common the use of the word pride is in our vernacular. Specifically, I thought of how I've told my children over the years that I am proud of them. It's important to share love, affirmation and positive reinforcement with our children, but my transformational understanding of pride revealed to me that such an utterance revealed that I was taking pride in my children for their performance or accomplishments. Instead, I considered the following affirmations:

It makes my heart happy to see the success that you experienced as a result of …

or

Isn't a great feeling to experience the results of the effort you put into …

or

I think the Lord has blessed you with the ability to
_____, and I look forward to seeing how God will
develop it, and how you can use it to serve God and others.

4. Wisdom and Insight

Logos

> For, "Who can know the LORD's thoughts?
> Who knows enough to teach him?" But we
> understand these things, for we have *the
> mind of Christ*. (1 Corinthians 2:16 NLT;
> emphasis mine)

> The person without the Spirit does not
> accept the things that come from the Spirit
> of God but considers them foolishness,
> and cannot understand them because they
> are *discerned only through the Spirit*. (1
> Corinthians 2:14 NIV; emphasis mine)

> I meditate on your precepts and consider
> your ways. I delight in your decrees;

> I will not neglect your word. (Psalm
> 119:15–16 NIV)

What Are Your Rhema Takeaways?

A believer's identity in Christ provides an understanding of God's will and ways that is unknown to those who have not embraced Jesus Christ as Savior. This is because believers have the indwelling of the Holy Spirit—the Helper mentioned in John 14. The Holy Spirit helps believers to comprehend Scripture. It's incumbent upon believers to read God's Word in order for wisdom to develop. The amount of wisdom a believer develops is proportional to the time spent studying, internalizing and actively applying God's Word to situations and experiences in life.

Logos

> Do not conform to the pattern of this world, but be transformed by the renewing of your mind. Then you will be able to test and approve what God's will is—his good, pleasing and perfect will. (Romans 12:2 NIV)

> The **secret** of the LORD *is* with those who *fear** Him, And He will show them His covenant. (Psalm 25:14 NKJV; emphasis mine)

(*It may be helpful to note that "fear" in this context refers to a reverence for God and His holiness.)

What Are Your Rhema Takeaways?

When we develop an appreciation and respect for God's will and ways as opposed to the messages of secular culture, we'll develop our own spiritual barometer that will help us to discern right from wrong. Discernment is a unique and valuable form of wisdom that all believers can develop simply by learning and heeding God's Word.

Logos

> The law of the LORD is perfect, refreshing the soul. The statutes of the LORD are trustworthy, **making wise the simple**. (Psalm 19:7 NIV; emphasis mine)

> 'Call to me and I will answer you and tell you great and unsearchable things you do not know.' (Jeremiah 33:3 NIV)

What Are Your Rhema Takeaways?

God's Word is enlightening and refreshing; God reveals things to those who respect and honor Him as Lord; and

God invites us to seek Him and promises to share insights that were previously unknown.

ENDURING BENEFITS OF A BELIEVER'S IDENTITY IN CHRIST

While our spiritual growth is a developmental process, God is steadfast in His character and in the fulfillment of His promises to believers. Thus, believers have enduring benefits when they align themselves with Jesus Christ. Included below are several of those blessings.

1. His Investment in Us

Logos

> being confident of this very thing, that he who began a good work in you will perfect it until the day of Jesus Christ: (Philippians 1:6 ASV)

> And we know that in all things God works for the good of those who love him, who have been called according to his purpose. (Romans 8:28 NIV)

What Are Your Rhema Takeaways?

God understands the nature of our spiritual growth and development process, and His involvement in refining us is continual. He can redeem situations and work in the lives of those with contrite hearts to move them forward in a positive direction.

2. His Love for Us

Logos

> For I am convinced that neither death nor life, neither angels nor demons, neither the present nor the future, nor any powers, neither height nor depth, nor anything else in all creation, will be able to separate us from the love of God that is in Christ Jesus our Lord. (Romans 8:38–39 NIV)

What Are Your Rhema Takeaways?

While we may do things that impact our status with others and the way that others think of us, God's love for us through Jesus Christ is steadfast and enduring.

3. A Firm Foundation

Logos

> Therefore everyone who hears these words of mine and puts them into practice is like a wise man who built his house on the rock. The rain came down, the streams rose, and the winds blew and beat against that house; yet it did not fall, because it had its **foundation** on the rock. (Matthew 7:24–25 NIV; emphasis mine)

What Are Your Rhema Takeaways?

God provides a solid, structurally sound foundation for weathering the storms of life to those who choose to embrace His will and ways. This foundation resists erosion, shores up believers, and stands the test of time. What comprises the foundation?

4. Peace

Logos

> I have said these things to you, that in me you may have peace. In the world you will have tribulation. But take heart; I have overcome the world." (John 16:33 ESV)

> I am leaving you with a gift—peace of mind and heart. And the peace I give is a gift the world cannot give. So don't be troubled or afraid. (John 14:27 NLT)

What Are Your Rhema Takeaways? (For full context for the verses above, you may wish to read all of John 16.)

The peace that God provides through Jesus Christ and His plan for salvation and redemption provide believers with enduring hope and comfort.

5. Intercession

Logos

> For I gave them the words you gave me
> and they accepted them. They knew with
> certainty that I came from you, and they
> believed that you sent me. ***I pray for them***. I
> am not praying for the world, but for those
> you have given me, for they are yours.(John
> 17:8–9 NIV; emphasis mine)

What Are Your Rhema Takeaways?

Jesus intercedes for us! The word 'pray' is not conveyed in
the past tense. It's present tense. It's on-going.

The Charge

The following verse is highlighted in my Bible with a note beside it that says (unattributed) the following verse was one of Mother Teresa's favorites: Or do you think lightly of the riches of His kindness and restraint and patience, not knowing that the kindness of God leads you to repentance? (Romans 2:4 NASB) The purported knowledge of her appreciation for that verse resonates with me because when I consider the grace and mercy that God freely extends to me and anyone who believes in Jesus Christ as Savior, I am motivated to share the good news with others and to live a life that is pleasing and honoring to Him. God's Word shares a call to action with those who understand and place their identities in Christ.

Logos

> the eyes of your understanding being enlightened; that you may know what is the **hope of His calling,** what are the riches

of the glory of His inheritance in the saints, (Ephesians 1:18 NKJV; emphasis mine)

But you are a chosen people, a royal priesthood, a holy nation, God's special possession, that you may **declare the praises of him who called you out of darkness into his wonderful light.** (1 Peter 2:9 NIV; emphasis mine)

What Are Your Rhema Takeaways?

The **immediate, transformational and enduring** blessings that accompany the choice to identify with Christ are bountiful and are meant to be shared. Believers should share what God has done as well as give God the glory for it.

Logos

Therefore, we are **ambassadors for Christ**, God making his appeal through us. We implore you on behalf of Christ, **be reconciled to God.** (2 Corinthians 5:20 ESV; emphasis mine)

What is Your Rhema Takeaway?

As believers, we have a sphere of influence in which we interact with others. We represent God well when we choose to address or change things in our lives that misrepresent or dishonor Him. The world is watching, so make sure you practice what you preach and set a good example.

Logos

> For we are God's handiwork, created in Christ Jesus to do good works, which God prepared in advance for us to do. (Ephesians 2:10 NIV)

We have work to do! As new creations in Christ, God has equipped us with gifts to serve Him and build His Kingdom. Have you wondered what kind of work or contributions the Lord wants you to do or make?

Logos

> Do you not know that your bodies are temples of the Holy Spirit, who is in you, whom you have received from God? You are not your own; you were bought at a

price. Therefore honor God with your bodies. (1 Corinthians 6:19-20 NIV)

What Are Your Rhema Takeaways?

How have I disrespected my body? Drinking too much on occasion, not eating well, not exercising, and not controlling my tongue are just a few things that come to mind. When I consider God's view of my body, as the temple of the Holy Spirit, I am intrinsically motivated to have more respect for its care and use.

What Are Your Rhema Takeaways?

Logos

Therefore, since we are **surrounded by such a great cloud of witnesses**, let us throw off everything that hinders and the sin that so easily entangles. And let us **run with perseverance t**he race marked out for us, f**ixing our eyes on Jesus, the pioneer and perfecter of faith.** For the joy set before him he endured the cross, scorning its shame, and sat down at the right hand of the throne of God. (Hebrews 12:1–2 NIV; emphasis mine)

I have told you these things, so that in me you may have peace. In this world you will have trouble. But take heart! **I have overcome the world**. (John 16:33 NIV; emphasis mine)

What Are Your Rhema Takeaways?

We have inspirational support to encourage us in our faith journeys. Shake off whatever is holding you back from growing your faith, serving or honoring God. Look to God for help. Keep your eyes on the prize of God's kingdom. He understands the difficulties of this world. Jesus suffered greatly, but He faithfully fulfilled God's plan, resulting in eternal life in the presence of God.

Dig Deeper

Who do you think comprises the cloud of witnesses mentioned in Hebrews 12? Pose that question and Google it to find a biblically-based commentary that may increase your understanding.

Logos

> After this I looked, and behold, a great multitude that no one could number, from every nation, from all tribes and peoples and languages, standing before the throne and before the Lamb, clothed in white robes, with palm branches in their hands, (Revelation 7:9 ESV)

What Is Your Rhema Conclusion?

The Kingdom of God will be filled with all different types of people from all over the world. Their common denominator will be their personal choices to place their identities in Jesus Christ. The blessing of such an eternal citizenship and fellowship is why identity in Christ transcends all other forms of identity.

Notes

Praise forever to the King of kings.

About the Author

After working in the non-profit sector for more than 25 years, Amy is grateful to be experiencing a season of life in which she can devote more time to writing and sharing what she has learned from her involvement in several ministries and Bible studies. Her passion is to share God's Word in simple, accessible, and culturally relevant ways.

Printed in the United States
by Baker & Taylor Publisher Services